BRITISH HISTORY
The HANOVERIANS
1714-1837

Kingfisher

KINGFISHER
An imprint of Larousse plc
Elsley House, 24-30 Great Titchfield Street,
London W1P 7AD

Material in this edition previously published by Grisewood & Dempsey Ltd in
Children's Illustrated Encyclopedia of British History in 1992

This revised, reformatted and updated edition published by
Kingfisher in 1997

2 4 6 8 10 9 7 5 3 1

A CIP catalogue for this book is available from the British Library

ISBN 0 7534 0098 7

Printed and bound in Hong Kong

Consultant: David Haycock
Editor: James Harrison,
with Jean Coppendale and Honor Head
Designer: Edward Kinsey
Proofreader: John Hinman
Indexer: Yvonne Dixon
Cover design: Terry Woodley

CONTENTS

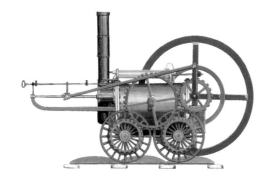

THE HANOVERIANS
(1714 – 1837)

THE HANOVERIAN KINGS ruled Britain for 123 years, presiding over the growth and loss of one empire (America) and, through exploration and trade around the world, the beginning of another. They ruled through two revolutions in America and France, which shook the established order and laid the foundations of the modern world. Britain itself underwent two other revolutions. The first was the Agricultural Revolution, which saw improved methods of growing crops, better livestock by selective breeding, and the invention of new farm equipment. Next came the Industrial Revolution, which saw the invention of machines to do work that had once been done by hand, and the harnessing of the power of steam to drive these machines.

Brighton Pavilion was rebuilt for George IV from 1815 to 1822 to look like an oriental palace.

George I

Above: George I (1714-1727) was 55 years old when he became King of England. He arrived from Hanover in Germany speaking no English, with two mistresses, two Turkish servants and several German advisers. A shy man, he proved to be a shrewd ruler.

Above: Robert Walpole, Britain's first prime minister, who advised both George I and George II from 1721 to 1742.

THE HANOVERIAN kings were descended from James I's daughter Elizabeth. She married the Elector Palatine Frederick V, who was chosen as King of Bohemia in 1619, defeated in battle the next year and exiled. His brief reign brought Elizabeth the nickname the Winter Queen. Their daughter, Sophia, married the Elector of Hanover. She was recognized as Queen Anne's heir when Anne outlived all of her 17 children, but Sophia died a few months before her, so the throne passed to Sophia's son, George.

George I was the great-grandson of James I. He was also, through his father, Elector of Hanover. This title meant that he was not only the King of Hanover, one of the states of the Holy Roman Empire, but also one of the nine German princes who had the right to elect the emperor whenever the imperial throne fell vacant.

GEORGE: THE GERMAN KING

George came to the English throne with very little knowledge about his new kingdom. He spoke no English: he and his ministers conversed in French. At first George relied on his Hanoverian advisers. He never became accustomed to England and remained isolated as he surrounded himself for most of his reign with fellow Germans.

Only in his later years did George begin to rely increasingly on the First Lord of the Treasury, Robert Walpole, who is regarded as Britain's first prime minister. Walpole was prime minister from 1721 to 1742, and later served George II.

THE AGRICULTURAL REVOLUTION

Farming methods had not improved since the Middle Ages. This changed dramatically in 1701 when a Berkshire gentleman farmer, Jethro Tull, invented the first farm machine which drilled holes in the soil and put a seed in each (until then sowing had always been done by hand). Tull also wrote about sowing crops in rows, or drills, with a gap between every two or three rows wide enough to allow his horse-drawn machine to be pulled.

In 1730 Viscount Townshend retired from government to his estates at Raynham in Norfolk. He improved on Tull's sowing methods by planting in rotation certain crops that in turn absorbed or put back different nutrients in the soil. Previously farmers would leave each field fallow (unused) every third year. One crop used by Townshend was turnips, from which came his nickname of Turnip Townshend. The turnips were used to feed cattle in the winter months, so not only was the soil improved by introducing turnips to the crop rotation cycle, but a better supply of meat was also ensured. A Leicestershire farmer, Robert Bakewell, improved the breeds of sheep, and paved the way for modern methods of stock breeding. Bakewell introduced the well-known breed of Leicester sheep, and England continued to dominate the supply of wool overseas. Such changes in farming methods in the 1700s became known as the Agricultural Revolution.

THE SOUTH SEA BUBBLE

In the 1700s many nobles and merchants made money by investing in British overseas trade in slaves, wool and other goods. The South Sea Company was a trading venture formed in 1711 promising profits from taking over all the trade in the Pacific Ocean. Shares were bought and sold for ten times their real value. Eventually the promises were found to be lies and in 1720 the South Sea Bubble – as the financial boom was called – burst. The company's shares dropped in value and thousands lost their savings.

Below: **Thomas Coke, Earl of Leicester, with some of his Southdown sheep. He increased his income almost ten times by introducing scientific methods of agriculture, and turned his estate at Holkham in Norfolk into an efficient model farm.**

- **1726** John Harrison invents "gridiron" (temperature proof) pendulum

- **1727** Death of George I: succeeded by George II (to 1760)

- **1729** Treaty of Seville, between Spain, France, Britain: Britain keeps Gibraltar. Scientist Stephen Gray discovers principle of electrical conduction. John and Charles Wesley start sect, later called Methodists

- **1730** Viscount Townshend begins experiments in agriculture. Edinburgh Royal Infirmary founded

- **1731** Treaty with Holy Roman Empire ends. Dutch set up rival East India Company. Spanish coastguards seize British ship *Rebecca*: her captain, Robert Jenkins has an ear cut off

- **1732** Walpole is offered No.10 Downing Street, London, as official residence; he is regarded as prime minister

- **1733** Walpole plans to introduce tax on wines and tobacco. National campaign against new taxes: Walpole withdraws them. John Kay patents his flying shuttle. George II's wife, Caroline, has Serpentine lake made in London's Hyde Park

- **1734** Jack Broughton, inventor of boxing gloves, wins championship of England from James Figg

- **1736** John and Charles Wesley organize groups of Methodists

- **1737** Licensing Act for London theatres: all plays to be censored by the Lord Chamberlain

- **1739** War of Jenkins' Ear with Spain (to 1748)

- **1740** War of the Austrian Succession (to 1748): Britain on Austrian side. Admiral Edward Vernon (Old Grog) makes first navy issue of rum diluted with water (called grog after him)

Jacobite Rebellions

THE CATHOLIC STUART KING James II had been overthrown in the Glorious Revolution of 1688. But many people still sympathized with the Stuart cause. They were known as Jacobites, from the Latin name *Jacobus* for James. In 1715 Scottish Jacobites rebelled, supported by a small revolt in the north of England. The 'Fifteen', as it was later known, was fairly easily suppressed, and James Edward Stuart, son of James II and called the Old Pretender, arrived from France to find the rising all but over. He soon went away again.

BONNIE PRINCE CHARLIE

George I was determined never to trust a Tory government, for he looked upon all Tories, who supported hereditary kingship, as being Jacobites.

In 1745, during the reign of George II, the Jabobites tried again. The Old Pretender's son, Charles Edward Stuart, the Young Pretender or Bonnie Prince Charlie, arrived in Scotland to raise his standard on his father's behalf. Only a few of the clans rose to join him.

At first Charles Edward and his men were successful. They captured Edinburgh and then marched south into England as far as Derby. The news of his arrival there caused a financial panic in London, but it was needless: Charles, finding no support for his cause in England, was already retreating.

Above: **Charles Edward Stuart (1720-1788) was the last serious Stuart contender for the British throne. He was a handsome young prince and known as Bonnie Prince Charlie. He was also called the Young Pretender, to distinguish him from his father who was known as the Old Pretender. But when Charles Edward died, aged 67, he had not fulfilled the promise of his earlier years.**

Right: **In 1715 at the battle of Sheriffmuir, 10,000 Jacobite troops led by the Earl of Mar fought against 4,000 English troops led by the Duke of Argyll. Both sides claimed it as a victory. Later that year the English Jacobites surrendered without a fight at Preston in Lancashire.**

THE BATTLE OF CULLODEN

On April 15th, 1746 Jacobite clansmen supporting the Young Pretender were severely beaten at the battle of Culloden, a fight which lasted only half an hour. William, Duke of Cumberland, George II's son, pursued the Scottish troops without mercy. Charles escaped to France and stern action was taken against the Highlanders. Many chiefs were executed and the clans were banned from wearing tartan or playing bagpipes.

FLORA MACDONALD

After the disaster of Culloden Moor, Charles Edward was a wanted man, hunted throughout the Highlands. But although the government put a price of £30,000 on his head, a great fortune in those days, none of the clansmen of the western Highlands betrayed him. Charles remained a fugitive for five months before a French ship picked him up and took him to safety.

During this time Charles was aided by many people, including Flora Macdonald, who became a Scottish heroine. She helped him to travel to the island of Skye disguised as her Irish maid. Flora was later arrested and jailed in the Tower of London, but was later freed by an Act of Indemnity in 1747. She married, and emigrated to North Carolina in America. Flora Macdonald eventually returned to Scotland in 1779.

Left: **During the 'Fifteen' Jacobite rebellion of 1715, the rebels who supported the Old Pretender, James Edward Stuart, were defeated by the English at Preston.**

Below left: **In the 'Fifteen' rebellion, battles were fought at Sheriffmuir and Preston. The 'Forty-five' rebellion saw battles at Prestonpans and Culloden.**

Below right: **At the battle of Culloden in 1746, the Jacobites were defeated by English troops led by the Duke of Cumberland.**

FOCUS ON THE BANK OF ENGLAND

Originally established to help finance the wars against the French in 1694, the Bank of England became a stable source of money for the government. Until George II's reign it was located in the Grocer's Hall, east London. It moved to its current site at Threadneedle Street in the City of London in 1734.

Above: **George II (1727-1760) was advised by prime minister Robert Walpole (who had also served George I), and later by William Pitt, the Elder, whose skills he came to appreciate, especially with victory in the Seven Years War.**

George II

GEORGE II SUCCEEDED his father in 1727 but, unlike his father, George could speak English. He was well advised by Robert Walpole, the first British prime minister, for the first 15 years of his reign. He was also influenced by his wife, Queen Caroline.

George had been a soldier all his life, serving under the Duke of Marlborough at the battle of Oudenarde in 1708 when Britain was dragged into a series of European wars. At the age of 60 he commanded the English and Hanoverian forces that won the battle of Dettingen in 1743, in the War of the Austrian Succession. George II was the last English monarch to appear on a battlefield.

George II's reign also saw the end of the Jacobite Rebellions and the start of the Seven Years War.

THE SEVEN YEARS WAR

The Seven Years War (1756-1763) was a conflict fought worldwide. It was fought between Britain and France for colonial possessions in America and India; and between Prussia, supported by Britain and Hanover, against an alliance of Austria, France, Russia and Sweden in Europe. Spain became involved as an ally of France.

The British conduct of the war was masterminded by the prime minister, William Pitt. He was known as Pitt the Elder to distinguish him from his son, William Pitt the Younger (also a prime minister).

Above: **Joseph Brant (1742-1807) was a Mohawk. When he was 12 years old he fought with the British against the French in North America in the war of 1754 over disputed boundaries. His Mohawk name was Thayendanega, but when he became friends with an English official he was given an English name and education.**

- **1750** First local cricket club formed at Hambledon, Hampshire. Jockey Club founded. Westminster Bridge completed

- **1751** Calendar change: January 1 declared to be New Year's Day in England (it was previously March 25), as in Scotland and the rest of Europe. Frederick, Prince of Wales, dies. Robert Clive leads British troops to victory against French at Arcot in India

- **1752** Britain adopts Gregorian Calendar: 11 days are dropped

- **1753** Surveyor George Washington is posted to drive the French out of Ohio, America. Newmarket races established

- **1754** French and British at war over boundaries in North America. Washington surrenders to French at Fort Necessity

- **1755** Royal and Ancient Golf Club, St Andrews, founded. French defeat British at Fort Duquesne (now Pittsburgh)

- **1755** Samuel Johnson publishes his great *Dictionary*

- **1756** Black Hole of Calcutta: many Britons are imprisoned in tiny room; 123 die. Seven Years War against France begins

- **1757** Robert Clive defeats ruler of Bengal at Plassey, and retakes Calcutta. Sankey Navigation canal built, linking St Helens coalfield to Mersey

- **1758** George Washington takes Fort Duquesne (Pittsburgh). Robert Clive becomes Governor of Bengal

- **1759** Battle of Quebec: British conquer Canada. British Museum opens

- **1759-64** Bridgewater Canal built

- **1760** Death of George II: succeeded by grandson, George III (to 1820). Clive leaves India; becomes Member of Parliament.

Left: **An English official in India is transported by elephant, and accompanied by an armed Indian escort. The British extended their influence in India after the East India Company's army fought the French with their Indian allies. In 1757 Robert Clive, an employee of the company, led the army to victory at Plassey against the Indian ruler of Bengal which was one of the richest areas of India. Clive later became Governor of Bengal and helped to establish British rule in India.**

Pitt the Elder was rewarded for his successes in the war with the title Earl of Chatham.

The Seven Years War spilled over into North America with border disputes between British and French colonies. These conflicts are often called the French and Indian Wars. The French had early successes, but were decisively beaten when a British force under General James Wolfe captured the French city of Quebec in a night assault in 1759. The battle lasted less than 15 minutes – Wolfe and the French commander, the Marquis de Montcalm, were both killed – but victory against the French helped to secure Canada for the British empire.

CLIVE AND INDIA

The Seven Years War extended to India where the British East India Company had much influence. The company had been formed originally in 1600 to compete with the Dutch East India company for the spice trade. But it was later given the right to govern over British subjects in its overseas posts and make treaties with non-Christian powers, such as the various Indian rulers called Moguls. The East India Company's soldiers, commanded by one of its clerks, Robert Clive, fought against the French in India, capturing and holding the city of Arcot in 1751.

At Arcot Clive and his English army, with the added help of some Indian soldiers, resisted a siege for 53 days before the French finally gave up. This marked a turning point in the struggle between the French and English in India.

THE BLACK HOLE OF CALCUTTA

During the Seven Years War, Siraj-ud Daulah, the Nawab (ruler) of Bengal, tried to oust the French and the British from India. He began by capturing Calcutta from the British. In 1756 he took 146 prisoners, who were herded into a room about 4.5 by 5.5 metres. It was extremely hot and badly ventilated and only 23 of the prisoners came out alive. Clive, with an army of 3,000 men, defeated the Nawab at the battle of Plassey in 1757. Bengal passed into British rule.

THE PEACE OF PARIS

The Peace of Paris, signed on February 3, 1763, finally ended the Seven Years War between England and France for overseas territories, and restored various islands and coastal forts to their former owners. France lost all but a few small bases in India and, in North America, all of Canada and possessions east of the River Mississippi. From Spain, Britain gained Florida.

7

The Industrial Revolution

Left: The first steam engines were invented to drive pumps which could prevent flooding in mine pits. One of the most successful was invented by Thomas Newcomen in 1712. His engine was slow and noisy but the miners were thankful for it, and improvements were made to make the engines pump more quickly.

FROM THE 1730s manufacturing in England went through many changes. Before then most people worked on the land or at home, producing goods by hand or using simple machines worked by human or animal strength. All this changed dramatically with the invention of larger machines driven by water wheels and windmills and later by steam power.

The first steam engines were developed in the early 1700s and were used mainly for pumping water out of mines. In 1782 James Watt invented a steam engine which could drive the new machines being used mainly to help produce cotton and other textiles. Factories were built to help increase production. This change was called the Industrial Revolution, a process which continued well into the 20th century until the arrival of new technologies.

Left: During the Industrial Revolution many factories were built very quickly in the developing industrial centres. The ever-increasing drive to manufacture goods created appalling working conditions. In the textile mills, for example, women and children often worked 12 hours every day for a pitiful wage.

THE NEW FACTORIES

When people made hand-crafted goods, such as weaving cloth on hand looms, they did so mostly from home with simple machinery worked by hand or foot. Often the whole family would be involved. Now, in the new factories, people had to work to the orders of those who employed them. Factory conditions were noisy, dirty and dangerous. Women and children as young as 5 or 6 might work from 5 o'clock in the morning to 8 o'clock at night, 6 days a week.

POPULATION EXPLOSION

Between 1780 and 1851 the population of Britain increased from 13 million to 27 million, so there were a lot more people looking for work. Many flocked to the new mines, workshops and industrial cities, such as Manchester and Liverpool.

Before the growth of industry, people had lived in country towns and villages. There were only a few big cities, such as London and Bristol. But by 1851 more than half the population lived in cities, most in miserable conditions. Overcrowding became a problem with houses crammed together in streets with no running water or proper drains.

CANALS

A combination of things made the Industrial Revolution possible. Money for trade and investment was readily available from a well-run banking system. Above all, it was the improvement in transport for carrying goods across the country that really spurred development. James Brindley was one of the early canal builders. His first canal took coal from mines at Worsley into Manchester. It helped reduce the cost of coal and in the 1790s other towns also built canals. By 1800 there was a network of linked canals across the country.

On the seas, wooden and later iron steamships began to replace sailing ships for overseas trade. Roads, bridges and tunnels were greatly improved, while later the invention of long-distance railways gave Britain another vital transport network.

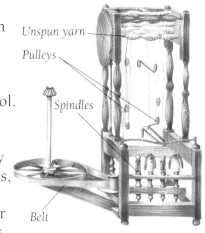

Unspun yarn
Pulleys
Spindles
Belt

Above: **James Hargreaves' spinning jenny of 1764 which allowed a worker to spin with several spindles at once. It was one of many ingenious and complicated machines invented during the Industrial Revolution. It altered work methods that had not changed for hundreds of years.**

Below: **Early 18th century weaving shuttles. On the right is a flying shuttle, invented by John Kay in 1733. Instead of being passed to and fro by hand, it flew on wheels. It greatly speeded up weaving.**

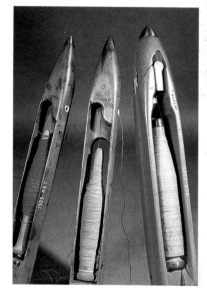

Left: **Canals were built throughout Europe so barges could carry heavy goods cheaply and easily. A single horse could pull a barge containing the same amount of coal that it would take over 60 pack-horses to carry. Canals were also better than bumpy roads for transporting delicate goods such as pottery. Pottery owner Josiah Wedgewood paid engineer James Brindley to build a canal from Stoke-on-Trent to the port of Liverpool.**

DISCOVERIES IN SCIENCE

Modern scientific ideas had been greatly boosted by the formation of the Royal Society in 1662, in Charles II's reign, to promote scientific research and discovery. British scientist Robert Boyle experimented with gases and founded the ideas for modern chemistry, while Sir Isaac Newton made the first mirror telescope and explained for the first time how the force of gravity kept the sun and the planets in orbit.

HADLEY'S SEXTANT

Isaac Newton died in 1727, but before his death he had also suggested adding a telescope to an existing navigational aid called the quadrant. This was to become the sextant invented by John Hadley in 1731. Hadley produced an instrument with which navigators could fix their position by the position of the stars and the sun. The sextant measures the height of a star above the horizon against a scale using mirrors and lenses. Knowing the height of the star above the horizon and the time of day, the navigator could plot his position.

HARRISON'S CHRONOMETER

Many great scientific discoveries and voyages of discovery would not have been possible without accurately made instruments such as the sextant. One of the great instrument makers was John Harrison who succeeded in 1759 in designing a watch – called the chronometer – which lost only five seconds during a two-month voyage to Jamaica.

Left: John Harrison invented the marine chronometer in 1735. The bottom dials read days, the left-hand dial minutes, the right-hand dial hours and the top dial seconds. For the first time sailors could measure their precise position at sea.

This was a vital invention because a captain had to know the exact time in order to work out his position at sea. Son of a Yorkshire carpenter, Harrison was self-taught and went on to build four chronometers which are now housed at the Royal Observatory in Greenwich. A prize of £20,000 had been offered for such an invention but the commissioners in charge of the fund would not release the money. George III decided to intervene personally to ensure that the prize money was paid in full to Harrison. Three years before his death in 1776, Parliament voted to pay 'Longitude' Harrison his just reward. His chronometer enabled a captain for the first time to pinpoint exactly where his ship was in the ocean even if there was no land in sight. The first captain to benefit from this invention was James Cook who called it "our trusty guide".

JAMES COOK

James Cook was the son of a farm labourer from Yorkshire. In 1755, during the French and Indian Wars, he joined the British navy and piloted Wolfe's boats to Quebec. Cook was quickly promoted because he showed great courage and skill as a navigator. Cook's navigational skills were so good that in 1768 he was chosen to sail the ship *Endeavour* to Tahiti with a group of astronomers on board. They wanted to study the planet Venus from the southern hemisphere.

Lenses

Mirror

Lens

Mirror

Scale

Left: **The sextant was first thought of by the great British scientist Isaac Newton but was first made by John Hadley in 1730. It is an instrument used as an aid to navigation. A sailor can determine his latitude (position relative to the equator) at sea by measuring the angle between a star or planet and the horizon, but the weather has to be clear.**

BOTANY BAY

On his way back from Tahiti, Cook sailed right round New Zealand, charting its coasts, and landed eventually at Botany Bay in southeast Australia. Naturalists on board picked 1,300 flowers in Botany Bay that Europeans had never seen before, and carefully sketched them as a record to bring back to Britain. The natural harbour on which Sydney is situated, Cook named Port Jackson, after Sir George Jackson, Secretary of the Admiralty.

FURTHER VOYAGES

On a second voyage from 1772 to 1775, Cook discovered Antarctica as well as returning to New Zealand and the New Hebrides for further exploration. Cook died during his third voyage in 1779. He was killed by angry Hawaiian islanders. Cook is famous for having been the first seaman to introduce fresh fruit and vegetables to the crew's diet to prevent outbreaks of the disease scurvy, caused by lack of vitamin C. His aim in life was "not only to go farther than anyone had done before but as far as possible for man to go".

Above: **George III (1760-1820) was very interested in farming, and he particularly liked his nickname, Farmer George. He also took an interest in science and championed John Harrison's invention of the chronometer which in turn enabled Captain Cook to make his voyages from 1768 to 1779.**

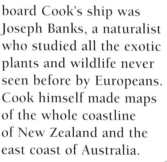

Below: **Captain Cook arrives in Tahiti in the Pacific Ocean. His voyages were those of scientific discovery. With him was a group of astronomers who wanted to observe the stars from the southern hemisphere. Another scientist on** board Cook's ship was Joseph Banks, a naturalist who studied all the exotic plants and wildlife never seen before by Europeans. Cook himself made maps of the whole coastline of New Zealand and the east coast of Australia.

- **1760** Botanical Gardens at Kew open

- **1762** War against Spain declared. Tory Earl of Bute becomes prime minister

- **1763** Peace of Paris ends the Seven Years War: British proclamation provides government for Florida, Grenada and Quebec

- **1763** Tory ministry falls: Whigs take office under George Grenville. John Wilkes attacks King's Speech and is arrested

- **1764** Wilkes expelled from Commons. James Hargreaves invents the spinning jenny. Clive returns to India to govern Bengal

- **1765** Stamp Act imposes further taxes on American colonies; challenged in Virginia. Clockmaker John Harrison perfects his chronometer which enables navigators to pinpoint exactly where they are. Captain Cook later uses it on his famous voyage to Australia

- **1766** Stamp Act repealed. Pitt the Elder, now Earl of Chatham, forms new government. John Byron takes the Falkland Islands for Britain. Theatre Royal, Bristol opens (oldest in Britain still in use)

- **1767** Tea, glass, paper and dyestuffs taxed in American colonies

- **1768** James Cook begins first voyage of discovery to the Pacific Ocean. Royal Academy founded

- **1769** Richard Arkwright invents the spinning frame. Wilkes expelled from Commons

- **1770** Parliament repeals all but tea tax in American colonies. Cook discovers Botany Bay

- **1771** Spain agrees to cede Falklands to Britain after near war. First edition of *Encyclopedia Britannica*

American Colonies

THE BRITISH COLONIES in North America largely looked after their own affairs and made their own laws. But Britain controlled their overseas trade, and limited what they could manufacture. In practice, however, the restrictions on manufacturing were often quietly ignored.

Trouble began when the British conquered the French colonies in North America, and decided they had to keep a British army on the continent to ensure the safety of the colonies against a possible French rebellion.

HATED TAXES

The British government also decided to tax the colonists to pay for this army. Successive attempts to tax sugar and imports of lead, paint, paper and tea to America met with fierce opposition, as did a stamp tax on all legal documents and newspapers. The colonists stated that they should not be taxed by a parliament where they were not represented.

All taxes except the one on tea were lifted, but an attempt by the British to make sure that only British-imported tea was drunk led to the Boston Tea Party in 1773, in which a group of colonists, disguised as Native Americans, threw a cargo of tea from three British ships into Boston Harbor.

Above: **The Boston Tea Party. On December 16th, 1773, about 100 colonists dressed as Native Americans tipped 342 chests of tea into Boston Harbor. They were protesting against a tax placed upon imported tea by the British government. The harsh British response drove the colonists to rebellion.**

Left: **This picture shows a detail from the painting *The Declaration of Independence* by John Trumbull. On July 4th, 1776, representatives of the 13 American colonies met in Philadelphia. The Americans standing are John Adams, Roger Sherman, Robert Livingstone, Thomas Jefferson and Benjamin Franklin.**

● **1772** Warren Hastings appointed Governor of Bengal. Lord Chief Justice, Lord Mansfield decides a slave is free on landing in England. Daniel Rutherford discovers nitrogen. James Watt improves steam engine to drive factory machines

● **1773** Boston Tea Party; cargo of tea dumped in Boston Harbor

● **1774** Britain passes Coercive Acts to control colonies, and closes port of Boston. John Wilkes becomes Lord Mayor of London.

AMERICAN WAR OF INDEPENDENCE

This was one of the many incidents that led to the Revolutionary War in America from 1776 to 1783. The situation deteriorated rapidly, until the night when British troops, called redcoats, marched to Concord, Massachusetts, to seize a colonial supply of arms. Silversmith Paul Revere sped on horseback that night to warn fellow American colonists of the redcoats' advance. Armed colonists and British soldiers faced each other in the cold dawn light at Lexington, on the road to Concord. A shot was fired – described by the great American poet Ralph Waldo Emerson as "the shot heard round the world". No one knows who fired it, but the war, which lasted for eight long years, had begun.

DECLARATION OF INDEPENDENCE

On July 4, 1776 American patriots including Thomas Jefferson, Benjamin Franklin and John Adams, issued their world-famous Declaration of Independence in which they listed their grievances against George III. They began by stating that "All men are created equal, that they are endowed by the Creator with certain inalienable rights; that among them are Life, Liberty, and the pursuit of Happiness". It was read out publicly and copies were given to most of the colonists.

Britain tried to crush the rebellion. In New York a British army advanced against American troops which were led by George Washington. Washington and his troops retreated. France then recognized the independence of the United States and entered the war, followed by Spain and Holland. Britain now faced many enemies and was forced to make peace at the Treaty of Versailles in 1783.

Above: **General George Washington (far right) led the rebellious American armies to victory over the British in the American War of Independence. He eventually became the first President of the United States in 1789.**

Below: **The battle of Yorktown, Virginia. On October 17, 1781, the British army, led by General Cornwallis, surrendered to the American forces backed by the French. Britain had lost the war and the American colonies.**

- **1775** American War of Independence begins: British defeated at Lexington; British victory at Bunker Hill. James Watt perfects steam engine

- **1776** Adam Smith publishes *The Wealth of Nations*. British forces driven from Boston, but capture New York. 13 American colonies declare independence

- **1777** British victory at Brandywine. American victory at Saratoga. John Howard begins prison reform

- **1778** Britain declares war on France

- **1779** First steam-driven spinning loom. Spain declares war on Britain. James Cook killed in Hawaii. First cast-iron bridge completed at Coalbrookdale

- **1780** Henry Grattan demands Home Rule for Ireland. Gordon Riots (anti-Catholic) in London. Britain declares war on Holland. The Derby horse race founded

- **1781** William Herschel discovers the planet Uranus. British surrender at Yorktown

- **1782** Spain captures Minorca from Britain. Wilkes wins support of House of Commons

- **1783** Britain grants Ireland the right to pass her own laws. Treaty of Versailles ends the American War of Independence

Slavery

SLAVES were people who were bought, sold and owned by someone else, just like property. The Romans used slaves, and even the serfs of feudal times, who worked for nobles in return for a little land, really had no more freedom than slaves, even if they could not be bought or sold.

Left: Slaves worked at cutting and refining the sugar on plantations in many parts of the Caribbean. Some slave owners were prepared to work their slaves to death (which took six years on average) and then replace them, rather than feed and care for them properly. Many slaves tried to run away to freedom.

THE SLAVE TRADE

The trade of capturing and transporting slaves from Africa to work in the new American colonies began in the 1500s with the Spanish and Portuguese. In 1562, John Hawkins became the first English slave trader. By the middle of the 1700s more than 100,000 slaves were being transported in appalling conditions to North America or the Caribbean, to work on the cotton or sugar plantations. At least half of these slaves were carried in British ships which sailed from Bristol and Liverpool. The slave trade through these ports was one of the richest ever seen.

THE TRIANGULAR ROUTE

The route of the slave trade resembles a triangle: ships from Bristol or Liverpool sailed to West Africa with cargoes of iron goods such as guns; these goods were exchanged for slaves who had been captured by local slave traders. Packed with slaves, the ships then set sail across the Atlantic to the Americas where the survivors were sold at auctions. The now empty ships completed the triangle back to the British ports carrying sugar, cotton and tobacco from the colonies. British traders made vast profits while some twenty million slaves suffered life without freedom.

MOVES AGAINST THE SLAVE TRADE

Until the late 1700s most people had regarded the treatment of slaves with indifference. In fact many wealthy traders and colonists would bring back slaves with them as personal attendants. However, some believed that any slaves brought back to Britain were automatically emancipated (made free). By the end of the 1700s people, especially those who followed simple Christian beliefs, saw how cruel the slave trade was and denounced it.

WILLIAM WILBERFORCE

A society to suppress slavery was formed by William Wilberforce in 1787. Wilberforce was the Member of Parliament for Hull, a slave trade port, and a friend of William Pitt, the prime minister. Wilberforce persuaded Pitt to appoint a committee to look into conditions on board the slave ships. The results of the inquiry opened people's eyes to the horrors of slavery.

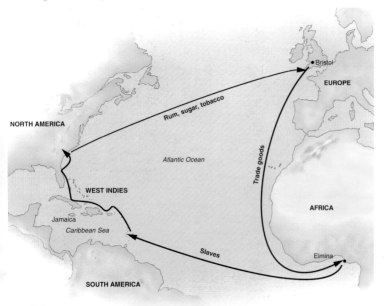

Left: The slave trade triangle. British goods were traded for African slaves. Slaves transported to America produced raw materials, such as cotton, tobacco and sugar-cane for use by British factories.

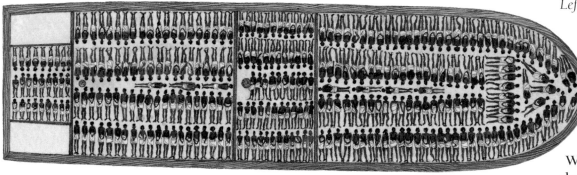

Left and below: Plans of the cruelly cramped conditions in which slaves were stowed on ships for the Atlantic run. The slaves could hardly move and were manacled in irons. William Wilberforce showed such plans to convince Parliament of the need to end the slave trade.

Above: William Wilberforce (1759-1833) fought for the abolition of slavery as a Member of Parliament. The slave trade was finally banned in 1807 in the British empire.

THE CASE OF JAMES SOMERSET

Another turning point in people's attitudes to slavery came when Granville Sharp fought in the courts to maintain that "as soon as any slave sets his foot on English ground, he becomes free". He selected the case of James Somerset, a slave from Virginia, to contest. The case was decided in favour of Somerset. At a stroke 14,000 people who were held as slaves in England were set free.

ABOLITION OF THE SLAVE TRADE

In Parliament, Wilberforce continued his campaign to halt the slave trade. Members of Parliament Charles James Fox and Lord Grenville passed a resolution in favour of abolishing the slave trade. The abolition of slavery became law in 1807. But employers and traders in the West Indies still wanted slaves and the trade continued secretly.

FREEDOM FROM SLAVERY

Wilberforce and his supporters formed the Anti-Slavery Society in 1823 to continue trying to ban slavery altogether. He began another long campaign to ban people from owning slaves, which would help ensure the end of any trading in slaves. While Wilberforce was ill and close to death, the Emancipation Act of 1833 was passed which ensured that slaves in the colonies would be freed. But it was not fully effective until the end of the 1830s. Former slave-owners in the British empire were paid £20,000,000 compensation. France and Holland passed similar acts. But slavery was not abolished in America until 1863.

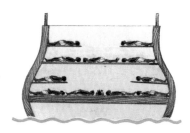

Below: Slaves working the treadmill in a Caribbean sugar plantation in the 1700s. They did this day in and day out and were whipped if they did not work hard enough. It is not surprising that many died from ill-treatment.

- 1783 Portland's coalition government is defeated: William Pitt the Younger forms a ministry. First paddle steamer crosses the English Channel

- 1784 General Election: Pitt wins a large majority in the House of Commons. India Act controls the East India Company

- 1785 Warren Hastings is recalled from India for bad administration. First balloon crossing of the English Channel. Daily Universal Register (now called The Times) is launched

- 1787 Sierra Leone founded as settlement for freed slaves. Edmund Burke impeaches Warren Hastings (trial 1788-1795)

- **1788** First fleet of European settlers arrives in Australia led by captain Arthur Philip; half are prisoners from Britain; settlement established in Botany Bay, New South Wales. George III becomes insane

- **1789** Mutiny aboard HMS *Bounty:* Bligh and 18 crew set adrift in open seas. George III recovers. George Washington becomes first American president

- **1790** Wolfe Tone founds the Society of United Irishmen. Firth-Clyde Canal completed. Pitt wins an increased majority in Parliament

- **1791** Ordnance Survey established. *The Observer* newspaper founded. Thomas Paine issues Part I of *The Rights of Man*

Revolutionary Years

GEORGE II'S GRANDSON became George III in 1760. He was the first Hanoverian king to be born and educated in England. He was to reign for 60 years, but from 1811 to 1820 he suffered such poor mental health that his son ruled as Prince Regent. George's reign witnessed great political and social upheavals.

WILKES AND LIBERTY

George's first prime minister, Lord Bute, was unpopular and faced the challenge of John Wilkes, a Member of Parliament, calling for freedom of speech. Wilkes attacked Bute and the king in his newspaper, *The North Briton*. For this Wilkes was sent to the Tower. A court judged that his privileges as a Member of Parliament exempted him from imprisonment except for treason or felony, and he was freed.

Wilkes's enemies had him expelled from the House of Commons, and he was tried in his absence for libel and outlawed. With the watchword of "Wilkes and Liberty!" he was twice more elected and expelled. Wilkes was also a keen supporter of the American colonists, again attacking the king and his ministers at every opportunity. Wilkes then turned to local government, and became alderman, sheriff and later Lord Mayor of London. In 1774 he was yet again elected to Parliament, and this time held his seat for 16 years. He died in 1797.

THE RIGHTS OF MAN

One of the leading revolutionaries of the 18th century was the agitator and pamphleteer, Thomas Paine. He was a friend of Benjamin Franklin, and went to America. There he wrote many pamphlets, including *Common Sense*.

Below: On July 14, 1789, the people of Paris attacked the Bastille, a fortified prison. The British government feared that revolutionary fervour would sweep into Britain.

Above: The guillotine, used during the French Revolution was nicknamed the national razor. It was invented by Dr Guillotin, a physician, in 1789. In Paris alone, 2,690 victims were guillotined in 1793 during the time called the Reign of Terror, while across France 40,000 died.

This pamphlet recommended the separation of the American colonies from Britain. Paine also served in the revolutionary forces. In 1787 he went to France, returning to England in 1791 to write *The Rights of Man*, a defence of the French Revolution which had begun in 1789.

Paine was promptly accused of treason, but before he could be tried he escaped to France. There he was made a French citizen, and served in the Convention. His outspokenness landed him in jail. He later returned to America in 1802, where he died in 1809 aged 72.

REVOLUTIONARY WARS

The French Revolution of 1789 was regarded with fear by many British politicians, because they thought the revolutionary movement might spread to Britain. The execution of the French monarch, Louis XVI, and his queen Marie Antoinette, in 1703, led Britain to became part of a coalition with Austria, Prussia, Spain, Portugal, Sardinia and the Netherlands against France. From 1793 to 1802 the French armies had many victories on land.

THE PRESS GANG

Although Britain depended on the navy for its safety, the sailors who served in its ships were treated very badly. This was the era of the cat-o'-nine-tails and ship's biscuits (which were often infested with beetles called weevils). Few men were willing to volunteer to join, so naval captains were allowed to send out groups of sailors called press gangs to drag any men between the ages of 18 to 55 on board their ships against their will. They were then forced to serve in the king's navy. This was known as impressment. Most sailors were conscripted by the press gangs. Once trained, their pay was only a few pence a day for ordinary seamen.

THE NAVAL MUTINIES

In 1797 the sailors serving in the fleet which was anchored at Spithead mutinied. They had asked for better pay and food, and the dismissal of about a hundred officers whom they considered too severe. After some negotiation their demands were met. The fleet at the Nore, near Sheerness on the River Thames, also mutinied, but their demands were more extreme. They did not get their way, and several of the ringleaders were hanged.

Above: **Sailors haul down the red flag on the** *Royal George* **during the Spithead Mutiny of 1797. They refused to set sail** again unless they were given one shilling (5p) a day more and better conditions. Agreement was finally reached.

MUTINY ON *THE BOUNTY*

Another very famous mutiny took place in 1789 on board the British ship HMS *Bounty* far away in the Pacific Ocean. The ship was captained by William Bligh to collect a cargo of breadfruit plants from Tahiti in the south Pacific. The crew enjoyed their stay at Tahiti and hated Bligh who was extremely harsh. Led by Fletcher Christian, they rebelled against Bligh rather than sail on.

Bligh and 18 loyal crew were set adrift on an open boat with no map and very little water. Bligh survived a journey of 7,000 kilometres. Several of the mutineers were executed but the rest eventually settled on the remote Pitcairn Island where some descendants still live today.

The Napoleonic Wars

THE BRITISH FLEET under Horatio Nelson finally destroyed the French navy at the battle of the Nile in 1798. At the battle of Copenhagen in 1801, Nelson was in desperate danger and was ordered to withdraw by his commander, but he put the telescope to his blind eye (which he had lost in a sea battle off Corsica) saying: "I really do not see the signal". He went on to destroy the Danish fleet, who were allied with the French.

During the French Wars from 1793 to 1802, one of the world's most famous generals had emerged from France, the Corsica-born Napoleon Bonaparte. Napoleon became Consul, then Emperor of France, and from 1803 to 1815 the wars between France and Britain and allied countries became known as the Napoleonic Wars.

Right: Admiral Horatio Nelson (1758-1805) lost the sight in one eye in 1794 and his right arm in 1797 in naval battles. He was killed at Trafalgar in 1805 and buried in St Paul's Cathedral.

Below: Nelson's signal to his fleet before the battle of Trafalgar was "England expects that every man will do his duty", and this decisive encounter stopped Napoleon's forces from advancing to invade Britain. They had been gathered at Boulogne on the French coast, waiting to cross over in barges. Nelson knew that if he could destroy the French fleet at Trafalgar there would be no invasion.

NELSON AND TRAFALGAR

In 1805 Napoleon, now Emperor of France, made great preparations for invading England. At the port of Boulogne, a flotilla of gunboats was ready to carry 150,000 soldiers over to England. Nelson returned from the West Indies to lead the British navy. In 1805 he won the memorable battle of Trafalgar, but was shot in the moment of victory.

Nelson died a few hours later, after saying the immortal words, "Thank God, I have done my duty". It is possible to see where he was shot and taken below deck on board HMS *Victory,* at Portsmouth Harbour in Hampshire. The life of a wartime sailor in the low-ceiling decks with the ear-splitting din of cannon-fire is brought to life vividly at this museum.

Left: The Duke of Wellington defended Britain successfully against Napoleon. After his victory at Waterloo he was given a hero's welcome and later became prime minister. He also gave his name to a type of boot and a style of cooking beef.

THE PENINSULAR WAR

The Peninsular War, so called because it took place in the Iberian Peninsula (which contains Spain and Portugal), was Britain's main contribution to the land war against Napoleon in Europe.

Spain was ruled by Napoleon's brother, Joseph, but its people, and the Portuguese, asked for Britain's help. Napoleon lost the Peninsular War, which he called the "Spanish ulcer" because it drained away armies and money he needed for his conquests elsewhere.

THE DUKE OF WELLINGTON

The hero of the Peninsular War was Arthur Wellesley, who became, as his victories mounted up, a viscount, a marquis, and finally Duke of Wellington. Napoleon's invasion of Russia was a failure, and defeat in Europe forced him into exile. In 1814 Wellington played a leading part at the Congress of Vienna, which tried to settle the future of Europe after Napoleon's exile. Representatives of all the major European powers wished to see their monarchies strengthened after years of revolution and war.

THE BATTLE OF WATERLOO

When Napoleon escaped from the island of Elba off the west coast of Italy and made himself emperor again in 1815, it was Wellington, aided by the Prussian field marshal, von Blücher, who defeated him at the battle of Waterloo in Belgium. Wellington held out with a smaller army against Napoleon by forming his infantry into squares which fired rapid volleys against French cavalry charges until the Prussian troops arrived. The British exiled Napoleon to the island of St Helena in the South Atlantic, where he died in 1821.

Above: **A scene from the the battle of Waterloo fought in Belgium on June 18th, 1815, when 45,000 died or were wounded.**

Below: **On June 22nd, 1815 Napoleon Bonaparte signed his second and final abdication, and was banished to St Helena where he died.**

- **1793** France declares war on Britain. Britain seizes Corsica and French settlements in India

- **1794** Lord Howe defeats French fleet in the English Channel. Britain takes Seychelles, Martinique, St Lucia and Guadeloupe from France

- **1795** Lord Fitzwilliam, Lord Lieutenant, fails to carry through Catholic emancipation in Ireland. Dutch surrender Ceylon (Sri Lanka) to Britain. Hastings cleared of treason. Methodists separate from the Church of England

- **1796** Spain declares war on Britain. Ireland put under martial law. Edward Jenner vaccinates against smallpox

- **1797** Rebellion in Ulster quelled. Naval mutinies at the Nore and Spithead

- **1798** Wolfe Tone's Irish rebellion quelled. Horatio Nelson wins naval battle of the Nile. Lord Wellesley becomes Governor-General of India. Thomas Malthus writes *Essay on the Principle of Population*. Wordsworth and Coleridge's *Lyrical Ballads* appear: beginning of the Romantic Movement

- **1799** Britain becomes first nation to introduce a national Income Tax

- **1800** Britain captures Malta. Combination Act forbids trades unions. Attempted assassination of George III. Royal College of Surgeons founded

- **1801** Act of Union: Ireland becomes part of United Kingdom; Union Jack adopted as official flag. Nelson wins naval victory off Copenhagen. British occupy Cairo. General Enclosure Act passed. Elgin Marbles acquired for Britain. Richard Trevithick builds a steam road carriage

- **1802** Peace between Britain and France. Thomas Telford builds roads through Highlands

● **1802** John Dalton produces his atomic theory and tables of atomic weights. Madame Tussaud arrives in Britain from France

● **1803** Britain declares war on France, beginning the Napoleonic Wars. Irish patriot Robert Emmet rebels: is captured and executed. Caledonian Canal begun. British penal colony in Van Diemen's Land (Tasmania) set up

● **1804** Spain declares war on Britain. Richard Trevithick makes first successful steam train. British use shrapnel against the Dutch in battle (first use ever)

● **1805** Battle of Trafalgar: Nelson dies defeating the French. Napoleon decides not to invade Britain

● **1806** British forces occupy the Cape of Good Hope in South Africa. Pitt the Younger dies. Sir Francis Beaufort designs his scale to measure wind force

● **1808** British army sent to Portugal: start of Peninsular War. British commander Sir John Moore killed at Corunna: succeeded by Arthur Wellesley, later the Duke of Wellington

WILLIAM PITT THE YOUNGER

William Pitt the Younger was the son of William Pitt the Elder and in 1783 became England's youngest prime minister. He was a brilliant speaker and favoured moderate parliamentary reform. But he fell out with the king on the issue of Catholic emancipation in 1801. He came back to power from 1804 to 1806. As prime minister he reduced Britain's debt by raising new taxes, including the country's first income tax. He also played a vital role in organizing Britain and the other European allies against Napoleon.

WARREN HASTINGS AND INDIAN RULE

In 1773 Warren Hastings became the first British Governor General of India. Many Indian princes fought among themselves, and Hastings had to quell the civil wars and make alliances with friendly Indian rulers to defend the East India Company's territories. With little help from home, Hastings was sometimes ruthless, especially in raising money to pay for protecting Indian allies. Corruption was rife in India, but Hastings' actions were singled out by his political enemies, led by Edmund Burke. On his return to England in 1785, Hastings was impeached for corruption, but cleared after a famous seven-year trial.

Below: **This working model, called "Tipu's Tiger", shows a tiger devouring a European. It was made for Tipu, Sahib of Mysore. Between 1767 and 1799 Tipu tried to resist British control of his lands in India with the support of the French.**

FOCUS ON THE BRITISH MUSEUM

One man's collection of treasures from around the world formed the basis of the British Museum – that of Sir Hans Sloane, an Irish-born physician of Scottish ancestry. Besides being a well-known doctor and naturalist, he was a man with wide-ranging interests. In 1753 Sloane left his collection to the nation on condition that the government pay his heirs £20,000. It was a generous offer – Sloane's

collection included 50,000 books and manuscripts, 23,000 coins and medals and 20,000 natural history specimens. Other collections already in public hands were added to Sloane's. The British Museum was rebuilt in the 1800s to make room for the vast collection of treasures now on display.

UNION WITH IRELAND

In 1801 the union of Britain with Ireland, a dream of English kings for hundreds of years, was finally brought about. The British Parliament was all for the union. The Irish Parliament hesitated, but it was a corrupt body, and when some of its Members were offered pensions, peerages and other inducements, a majority was persuaded to vote for union. Only a few Irish Members, headed by Henry Grattan, fought to the last against it.

EMMET: THE IRISH REBEL

Despairing of Ireland's future, many Irishmen looked to France for help. Among them was Robert Emmet. After visiting Napoleon in Paris, Emmet believed the French would soon invade England. He decided to start a rebellion to help the French and so liberate Ireland from British political control. However, the rebellion in 1803 was badly organized, and ended in complete chaos. Emmet was arrested, tried and hanged for treason outside the Church of St Mary's, in Dublin. Despite his failure, Emmet has been regarded as a young hero by Irishmen ever since.

THE CATHOLIC QUESTION

As prime minister, Pitt had also hoped to see a law passed to lift the ban on Roman Catholics holding public office, including membership of Parliament. But here he was opposed by George III. This obstinate monarch, hovering on the edge of insanity, believed that if he were to agree to such a step he would be breaking his coronation oath to uphold the Church of England. To avoid driving the king over the brink into madness by opposing him on the Catholic question, Pitt gave way. Catholic emancipation was delayed for almost 30 years.

As a result, Ireland was at first represented in the Union Parliament only by its Protestant minority, which tended to be of either English or Scottish descent. As Protestants and Catholics were fiercely opposed to one other, the situation in Ireland remained very troubled.

JOHN WESLEY AND THE METHODISTS

During the Hanoverian period, more and more people moved into the new industrial and mining towns, but often lost their churches and beliefs.

Above: **William Pitt the Younger, Britain's youngest ever prime minister, led the Tory government in 1783-1801 and again 1804-1806.**

Below: **John Wesley (1703-1791), founder of the Methodist Church.**

- **1810** Duke of Wellington forces the French army to withdraw from Portugal. Durham miners strike

- **1811** America bans trade with Britain. George III becomes permanently insane: his son George is appointed Prince Regent

- **1812** Wellington storms Ciudad Rodrigo. British capture Badajoz. Prime Minister Spencer Perceval is assassinated at the Commons. America declares war on Britain. Napoleon invades Russia but most of his army dies in bitter winter. Wellington enters Madrid. Henry Bell's steamship *Comet* sails on the River Clyder. Main streets of London lit by gas

- **1813** American troops force Britain to abandon entire Niagara frontier. The American warship *Chesapeake* is captured. Wellington routs French at Vittoria: King Joseph Bonaparte of Spain flees to France. American naval victory on Lake Erie. British take Fort Niagara. Elizabeth Fry begins prison visits

- **1814** Allies enter Paris. British burn city of Washington. Statute of Apprentices repealed. Treaty of Ghent ends war with America. Treaty of Paris ends war with France: Britain retains Mediterranean island of Malta. MCC first play cricket at Lord's

John Wesley, who had once been a clergyman in the Church of England, changed this. He decided to take religion to these working people. From 1738, he travelled round the country on horseback, preaching over 40,000 sermons in the open air to the vast crowds which came to see him. Wesley believed the Church had become lazy and remote. His followers became known as Methodists because they followed a stricter method of prayer and study. In 1804, the Methodists split away from the Church of England.

Arts and Architecture

Theatre had thrived under Charles II with witty and satirical plays known as comedies of manners. During George III's reign, Oliver Goldsmith's comedy *She Stoops to Conquer* (1773), Richard Sheridan's *School for Scandal* (1777) and *The Rivals* (1775) continued the tradition – all three plays are still performed today.

SAMUEL JOHNSON

Dr Samuel Johnson established himself as the most famous literary figure of this period with his *Dictionary of the English Language* (1755). Johnson was also the subject of one of the greatest English biographies, *The Life of Samuel Johnson* (1791), written by his friend James Boswell. Among Johnson's friends were David Garrick, a great Shakespearean actor of his day (the Garrick Theatre in London is named after him), and Sir Joshua Reynolds, the painter, and first President of the Royal Academy. Johnson's loathing for the journalist and Member of Parliament John Wilkes was well known though the two men did meet and exchange views.

ROBINSON CRUSOE AND GULLIVER

Novels became very popular in the 18th century. *Robinson Crusoe* by Daniel Defoe was published in 1719, and many people regard it as the first successful English novel. It tells the story of a man who is being shipwrecked on a desert island, and is based partly on the true-life adventures of a traveller called Alexander Selkirk. Other famous novels of the period include Jonathan Swift's

Above: **The Elgin Marbles after their installation in the British Museum. They were brought by the Earl of Elgin from Greece to England between 1803 and 1812. They were claimed back by Greece in the 1990s, but Britain disputed the claim and they remain in the British Museum.**

Gulliver's Travels, which is a satire, or biting comic criticism of the way human beings live. Written in 1726, it describes four imaginary journeys by a ship's doctor named Gulliver: first to Lilliput where everyone is tiny, then to Brobdingnag where the people are giants, and finally to a country ruled by talking horses far more gentle and intelligent than humans. In 1760 Laurence Sterne wrote *Tristram Shandy,* a comic novel which expressed the author's own views on life using the technique of flashbacks and with less concentration on the plot.

The writer Jane Austen carried the novel's popularity into the 1800s.

Left: **The Haywain by John Constable (1776-1837), one of Britain's finest landscape painters. Many of his paintings showed scenes of Suffolk and Hampshire country life. His style was to record real places under different lighting and weather conditions. *The Haywain* shows a wagon crossing the River Stour near Flatford Mill in Suffolk.**

Above: **Jane Austen wrote romantic stories about attractive heroines and observed English society with a wry humour and insight. Her novels include *Pride and Prejudice* and *Sense and Sensibility*.**

The seventh child of a Hampshire clergyman, Jane Austen wrote witty novels with attractive heroines searching for ideal husbands. Today her novels such as *Pride and Prejudice* and *Sense and Sensibility* have been turned into highly successful films and television series. Her house at Chawton is a now a museum containing many of her personal effects.

Poetry also enjoyed something of a golden age with William Wordsworth, George Byron, John Keats and Robert Burns, the national poet of Scotland, among the leading poets in what was called the Romantic movement. Poets took British people, places and nature as a source rather than looking to classical Greece and Rome for inspiration. They also wrote using a simpler style of language that many more people could understand and enjoy.

ENGLISH PAINTING

In the 1700s a type of painting known as the English School emerged. Thomas Gainsborough became a fashionable society portrait painter who painted famous personalities of the time and was commissioned by wealthy businessmen to paint family portraits.

Right: **German-born George Frederick Handel worked for George I and George II. His most famous works were oratorios, a type of opera with choral singing and stories taken from the Bible, such as** *Messiah* **(1741). Other works include** *Music for the Royal Fireworks* **which accompanied a great firework display in London's Hyde Park to celebrate peace with France in 1748. English classical music developed dramatically in what is known as the Baroque period (1600s-1750s).**

In 1689, Henry Purcell produced *Dido and Aeneas*, often considered as the first English opera. Purcell wrote music for the Church, Court and the theatre.

Two of the greatest landscape painters to emerge at this time were John Constable and J.M.W. Turner, while George Stubbs studied and painted superb horses. William Hogarth depicted startling and often cruel scenes of London street life, and Thomas Rowlandson made fun of society with his caricatures (cartoons).

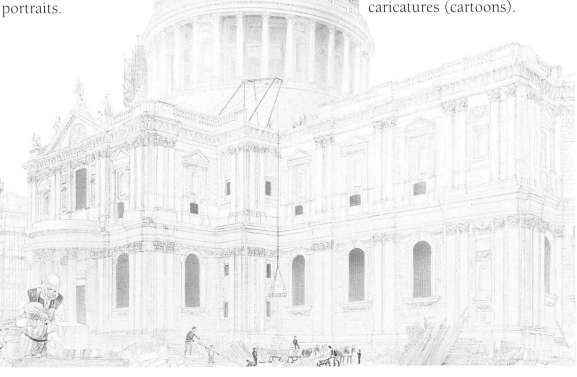

Left: **St Paul's Cathedral, London, was completed by Christopher Wren in 1710. He had introduced the new style of Baroque architecture from Italy, and it would continue under the Hanoverians. Sir John Vanbrugh's Blenheim Palace in Oxfordshire (1705-1724) is another great example of English Baroque architecture.**

The Age of Transport

T HE IMPROVEMENT OF ROADS and the building of bridges and tunnels in the 1700s and 1800s made the transport of goods and people much easier then ever before. Nobles and businessmen alike invested their wealth from slavery and other overseas trade into general improvements and inventions.

IMPROVEMENT TO ROADS

Most of the Roman roads had been allowed to fall into disrepair and many other roads had become dirt tracks again. From the mid 1700s, however, these roads were mended and new ones built. One of the most remarkable road builders was John Metcalfe, who was blind. He would feel the surface of the road to make sure it met his requirements.

A Scotsman, John Macadam, introduced the tarmac road surface which is still used today. Prisoners and people from workhouses would break the stones into thousands of small chipped pieces of the same shape and size. These would then be flattened with a heavy iron roller and sprayed with tar.

The results were dramatic for regular road users and travellers: a stagecoach journey between London and Edinburgh that took two weeks in 1745, took only 2½ days by 1796. Road repairs and improvements were paid for by Turnpike Trusts, which raised tolls on everyone travelling on their new roads.

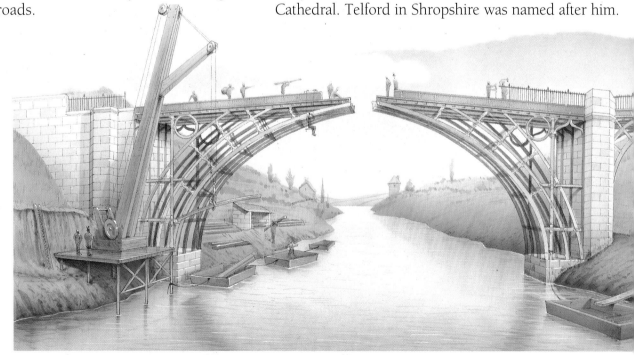

THOMAS TELFORD

The most famous road engineer, who also designed canals, bridges, lighthouses and tunnels, was Thomas Telford, another Scotsman. Telford believed that roads must be well-drained and built on a solid base of stone blocks – like the Roman roads. He built the famous road from London to Holyhead at the tip of Anglesey. In 1826 he completed the famous Menai Straits Bridge linking the north of Wales to the island of Angelsey, to carry his road. He was buried in Westminster Cathedral. Telford in Shropshire was named after him.

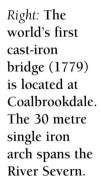

Right: **The world's first cast-iron bridge (1779) is located at Coalbrookdale. The 30 metre single iron arch spans the River Severn.**

Below: The heyday of horse transport was from the late 1600s to the mid-1800s. Stagecoaches took passengers, luggage and mail over long distances. With improvements to the roads, such journeys were now quicker and safer.

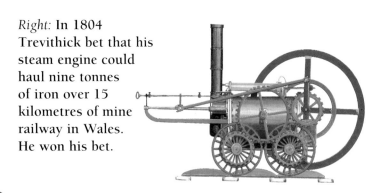

Right: In 1804 Trevithick bet that his steam engine could haul nine tonnes of iron over 15 kilometres of mine railway in Wales. He won his bet.

THE RAIL REVOLUTION

Railways became the main transport in the 1800s thanks to the invention of the steam locomotive by Richard Trevithick in 1804. This engine could move on rails under its own steam, pulling a train of wagons. Trevithick's locomotive proved that steam power could replace horses for freight and passenger transport. George Stephenson pioneered successful rail travel with his steam engine *Locomotion* in 1825. It was chosen to pull 12 wagons loaded with coal and 21 coaches with passengers along some 40 kilometres of track at the new Stockton and Darlington Railway – the first public steam railway in the world. On September 27th, crowds flocked to see the first trial run. A man on horseback rode in front with a red flag to make sure everyone kept well clear. But the loud hiss of steam scared the crowds and made the horse rear in panic! Nevertheless, this episode signalled the start of the railway age and at Darlington, in Durham, Stephenson's early engine can be seen standing on two original rails. In 1830 Stephenson supplied his locomotive *Rocket* for the new Liverpool and Manchester Railway. By 1841 there were more than 2,300 kilometres of track laid down in Britain.

Below: George Stephenson's *Rocket* won the 1829 trials to find the fastest locomotive for the Liverpool-Manchester Railway, the world's first all-steam public railroad. It reached a top speed of 58km/h.

THE WAR OF 1812

The War of 1812 between Britain and the United States broke out when the Americans objected to British ships blockading Europe during the Napoleonic Wars, and also stopping and searching American ships to look for British deserters. Britain announced it would lift the blockade for American ships.

But two days later, before word of this decision reached them, the Americans declared war. The war included the burning of the capital, Washington DC, by British soldiers. It was from this that the White House, the president's official home, got its name. It was blackened by fire and was painted white to conceal the damage, and its name and colour stuck. This inconclusive conflict ended with the Treaty of Ghent in 1814.

THE PETERLOO MASSACRE

Two of the major issues of the early years of the 19th century were the repeal of the corn laws, which kept corn and bread prices high, and parliamentary reform. On August 16, 1819 a crowd of 80,000 gathered in St Peter's Fields, Manchester, to hear a well-known radical speaker, Henry Hunt, demanding an end to the high price of bread and the reform of Parliament.

The local magistrates decided to arrest Hunt and other leaders of the demonstration, but instead of doing so before the crowd gathered, they waited until the people were listening to Hunt, in an orderly manner, and then sent in soldiers and cavalry with drawn swords. In the confusion that followed 11 people were killed and 400 seriously injured. The incident became known as the Peterloo Massacre, a belittling reference by the government's enemies to the battle of Waterloo. The name stuck and the government eventually changed a number of its policies – among them reducing public hangings and reforming the prisons.

PRINCE REGENT

Before George IV was crowned in 1820, he had already been ruler for nine years as Prince Regent on behalf of his father, George III, who had been declared insane. The period 1811 to 1820 is called the Regency period and it witnessed a dashing style in architecture, interior design and fashion.

Above: **A scene from the Peterloo Massacre. The mounted Yeoman officer, *(left)* is shouting "Chop 'em down, my brave boys… the more you kill the less poor rates you'll have to pay …"**

Below: **When George IV was Prince Regent he was a leader of fashion. The style of architecture, furniture and clothes at this time is labelled Regency.**

- **1815** Apothecaries' Act stops unqualified doctors practising. Humphry Davy invents the miner's safety lamp. Battle of New Orleans: British defeated by Americans. Corn law prohibits corn imports. Battle of Waterloo: Napoleon defeated and sent to St Helena. Income Tax ends

- **1816** Poverty in England causes emigration to America

- **1817** March of the Blanketeers: Manchester protesters, each carrying a blanket, demand political reform. *The Scotsman* newspaper founded

- **1818** Canadian-US border fixed at the 49th parallel. *Vulcan*: first all-iron sailing ship is built

- **1819** Britain gains Singapore. Peterloo Massacre: 11 killed when troops dispel mob in St Peter's Fields, Manchester. Working day for children cut to 12 hours in England

- **1820** George III dies: succeeded by Prince Regent as George IV (to 1830). First iron steamship launched

- **1821** *Manchester Guardian* founded

- **1822** Bottle Riots: Viceroy of Ireland attacked by Orangemen in Dublin. Royal Academy of Music founded

George IV

Left: **George IV (1820-1830) was secretly married to a Catholic widow, Mrs Fitzherbert, but this was not recognized officially and in 1795 he formally married Princess Caroline of Brunswick to help him pay off his debts.**

GEORGE IV WAS A COMPLETE contrast to his father. George III had been a simple, kindly man, known to his subjects as Farmer George because he took such an interest in agriculture and in his farm. He had also provided a moral example to his subjects through his virtuous way of life.

George IV was clever, generous, a patron of the arts and a good linguist. But he was also vain, a drunkard, a gambler and lazy, and faithless to his friends and his many mistresses. His conduct disgusted even his close friend, George Brummel, known as Beau Brummel because of the elegance of his dress and his excellent taste.

PEEL AND THE FIRST POLICE FORCE
It was the new home secretary, Robert Peel who helped bring about changes in capital punishment, prisons and law and order in the streets. After the Peterloo Massacre, Parliament realized it was wrong to send the army in to control crowds so they agreed to Peel's proposal in 1829, to set up a police force at first in London – providing it stayed unarmed. Within 30 years the "peelers" or policemen were on patrol in every town in the country.

FREEDOM FOR ROMAN CATHOLICS
The Catholic Relief Bill of 1829 lifted the ban that prevented Roman Catholics from sitting in Parliament or holding public office. The only posts barred to them after this were those of Lord High Chancellor or Lord Lieutenant of Ireland, and no Roman Catholic could succeed to the throne – a restriction which still applies today.

SMUGGLERS AND HIGHWAYMEN
In the Hanoverian period passengers on stage-coaches were at risk from attack by highwaymen such as Dick Turpin (who was caught and hanged in 1739). The law was also broken by smugglers who brought wine, tobacco, spirits, silk and sugar by boat to secret coves along the south coast to avoid customs duties. If they were caught, smugglers could face severe punishments, including hanging or being transported to Australia. Robert Peel introduced laws which helped to stop smuggling.

Above: **Smugglers brought valuable goods into creeks and coves by boat at night and avoided paying customs duties at ports.**

Right: **Until the police force became established around the country it was difficult to catch highwaymen who robbed on horseback with guns.**

Rich and Poor

IN THE 1700S AND 1800S, as people moved away from the countryside into the expanding industrial towns and pit villages, there was a widening gulf between the rich and the poor.

THE NEW INDUSTRIAL RICH

Prosperous traders and business-people lived in new elegant terraced houses like those that can still be seen in the fashionable Georgian spa town of Bath. George IV's Royal Pavilion was an exotic palace with extravagant interiors. It began life as a simple farmhouse and ended up looking like an Indian palace. George's palace helped transform a village called Brighthelmstone into the fashionable seaside resort of Brighton.

The rich enjoyed the new restaurants, theatres and meeting places such as the Pump Room and Tea Rooms in Bath. They ate rich foods such as partridge and swan and drank fine claret wine. Country landowners built grand stately homes set in magnificent parks, such as Harewood House in Yorkshire, decorated by Robert Adam in 1759 and landscaped by Capability Brown who was much in demand at this time. Castletown House, Celbridge, was completed in 1760 and is considered the finest Georgian house in Ireland.

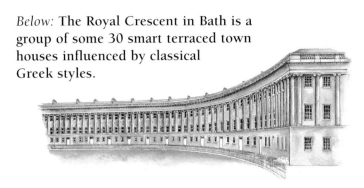

Below: **The Royal Crescent in Bath is a group of some 30 smart terraced town houses influenced by classical Greek styles.**

THE NEW INDUSTRIAL POOR

The poor workers lived in tiny houses, often built by the factory owners and close to the factories so the workers could start work there early. These houses were built back-to-back with outside earth toilets and one street pump to serve the whole row. Children could only play on the street, as there were no gardens or parks for them to play in. A family of three or four would be crowded into one room and slept in one bed.

Parts of the north-west such as Teeside, and South Wales, Birmingham and Glasgow saw the greatest growth in urban housing. The new factory chimneys belched out smoke which created the beginnings of industrial pollution.

Poorer people's food was nothing like the delicious fare consumed by the rich. They ate bread made from rye or barley, with cheese or butter.

Left: **Wealthy Georgian society in the Pump Room at Bath. The well-to-do liked to "take the waters" of this fashionable spa town with its hot springs. This scene is based on a famous cartoon which poked fun at the upper classes.**

HOW THE POOR SURVIVED

The poor could only afford the cheapest meat and usually put it into a broth. There were vegetables such as carrots, parsnips and cauliflowers to help give them some vitamins. To help ease their hard life, some people took to drinking an alcoholic spirit called gin which became popular in this period. It was very strong and people became very drunk. They also became violent and mob riots in London forced Parliament to try to limit sales of the drink. Beer and ales were also consumed in vast quantities by the poor.

For entertainment there was the blood sport of cock-fighting or boxing with boxing gloves or bare-knuckled. The rich preferred the sport of cricket.

CHILD LABOUR

Most boys and girls did not go to school but worked in the factories from the age of six. Small children were used to crawl into or under machines to mend broken threads or collect fluff, to prevent the machines from jamming – the work was hard and dangerous. Under the Poor Law, if a child did not have a mother or father or other relatives, they had to be brought up in the local poor-house. Factory owners bought many of these children for a small fee paid to the owner of the poor-house.

Under the Poor Law Act of 1834, workhouses were built to house homeless families and encourage them to pay their way through hard work. These were grim buildings run on very harsh rules.

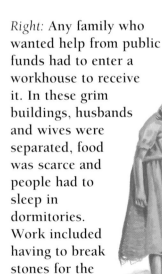

Above: **The evils of gin as drawn by the famous painter and engraver William Hogarth. He produced *Gin Lane* in 1751 and later painted a series of famous social scenes including the drunkenness and rioting of elections, which were very corrupt affairs.**

Right: **Any family who wanted help from public funds had to enter a workhouse to receive it. In these grim buildings, husbands and wives were separated, food was scarce and people had to sleep in dormitories. Work included having to break stones for the new roads.**

- **1823** Death penalty abolished for more than 100 crimes. Game of rugby football first played at Rugby School. Charles Babbage begins building the first forerunner of the computer

- **1824** Combination Acts of 1799-1800, banning trade unions, repealed

- **1825** Stockton and Darlington Railway opens: the first passenger-paying railway in the world

- **1827** Robert Peel reforms the criminal law code

- **1829** Corn law eases imports of corn. Roman Catholic Relief Act frees Catholics from discrimination

- **1829** Metropolitan Police established by Sir Robert Peel. British ban *suttee* (suicide by widows) in Hindu India. Rainhill locomotive trials: George Stephenson's *Rocket* wins. First horse-drawn omnibus in London provides cheap public transport. First Oxford-Cambridge Boat Race

- **1830** George IV dies: succeeded by brother William IV (to 1837). King's College, London, founded. Royal Geographical Society founded

- **1831** Reform battle begins: Lords reject Reform Bill. Electromagnetic induction discovered. Charles Darwin begins his voyage in HMS *Beagle*. James Clark Ross reaches North Magnetic Pole

- **1832** First Reform Act passed; it gives the vote to more middle-class men. Geological Survey begins. Durham University founded

- **1833** Britain reaffirms sovereignty over Falkland Islands. Factory Acts: no child under 9 to work in factories, 8-hour day for 9- to 13-year-olds. Slavery ends in British empire. First State grant for education

William IV

AS THE THIRD SON OF GEORGE III, William was not expected to become king and was not trained for the monarchy. Instead he began an early career in the navy as a midshipman at the age of 13, and later became a Rear Admiral and because of this he was known as the Sailor King.

THE DEMAND FOR REFORM

When William IV succeeded his brother George IV, who died in 1830, he was already 64. William's reign saw a period of great social, political and constitutional reform. The sufferings of the poor and their appalling working conditions, and the neglect of the lower and middle classes from proper representation in Parliament, had created an explosive situation. A second revolution in France, against the despotic King Charles X, led to the overthrow of the French monarchy for a second time. The demand for reform at home was strengthened by this event.

POLITICAL PARTIES

The main political parties were called Whigs and Tories: these terms had come into use in Charles II's reign as terms of abuse for political opponents. Whig was originally a name for Scottish cattle thieves; it was applied to those people who wanted to exclude James Stuart from the throne because of his Catholic sympathies. Tory was the name for a group of Irish bandits, and it was applied to those people who opposed James's exclusion from power.

Left: William IV (1830-1837) was a sailor from the age of 13. He was blunt, tactless and nicknamed Silly Billy. But as king he worked hard and his common sense ultimately led him to support the Great Reform Bill of 1832.

Both the Whig and Tory parties realized that something must be done to meet the rising resentment about rotten boroughs and the limits on who had the right to vote. But both parties were reluctant to surrender power enjoyed by the governing classes to which they both belonged.

The Whig party favoured some reform as a matter of justice and to prevent possible riots. The small Tory party led by the Duke of Wellington, and supported by the king, was opposed to sweeping reform simply to pacify the people. By about 1835 the Whigs had become known as the Liberals, and the small Tory party took on the name of Conservatives.

ROTTEN BOROUGHS

Despite the upheavals in agriculture and industry, which affected the way people lived and worked, and the warnings to the ruling classes of the French and American revolutions, Britain remained governed by the same sort of people who had governed the country since the 1700s.

FOCUS ON FARADAY

Michael Faraday (who lived from 1791 to 1867) was a scientist who is most famous for his research into the relationship between electricity and magnetism. He was offered a job by Sir Humphry Davy, the brilliant chemist who invented the miner's safety lamp. Faraday worked at the Royal Institution in London.

He discovered the dynamo (*left*) and his findings led to the invention of electric motors and generators. The farad, a unit to measure electrical capacity, is named after him. Faraday was also noted for giving talks which made scientific subjects easy to understand for ordinary people.

Members of Parliament represented the interests of the factory owners, not the interests of workers. There were no Members of Parliament from the new towns that had developed during the Industrial Revolution. Many Members belonged to ancient seats based on only a handful of electors. These rotten boroughs, as they were known, included Old Sarum in Wiltshire, which had no houses, and Old Dunwich, in Suffolk, which was mostly submerged by the sea. Pocket boroughs were those owned by weathy landowners who could evict tenants if they did not vote to their wishes.

Left: In 1833 the first of several Factory Acts was passed which safeguarded against child labour in textile mills. The Mines Act of 1842 stopped the employment of women and children altogether in coal mines. Christian men and women, such as Richard Oastler and Elizabeth Fry, helped to change the government's attitude to poor people.

REFORM OF PARLIAMENT

The Whigs came to power in 1830, after almost 50 years in the political wilderness, and at once set about the long overdue issue of parliamentary reform. Lord John Russell was a Whig who had supported Catholic emancipation and now led the movement for the Great Reform Bill of 1832. The First Reform Act of 1832 sorted out most of the redundant rotten borough seats, and local landowners lost their right to nominate, or suggest, Members of Parliament. The Act also created 455,000 new voters, by giving the vote to town's people occupying property worth at least £10 a year.

REFORMS IN WORKING CONDITIONS

In 1833 the new Parliament passed additional reform acts including the first Factory Act, by which children under 12 were not allowed to work in the factories for more than 8 hours a day, and women not more than 12 hours.

Left: English artist and engraver William Hogarth's cruel and vivid view of the corruption that went on during voting for a Member of Parliament. There was no secret ballot, voters had to declare their choice in public and so they were open to bribes and threats. In pocket boroughs, for example, which were voting areas owned by one wealthy person, voters could be evicted from their homes if they did not vote as the owner wanted them to. The First Reform Act of 1832 attempted to stop such practices.

The Factory Act further stated that children under nine were not to be employed at all. Later factory acts were to stop child labour altogether in all factories. They were also to stop the use of women and children in coal mines where they were employed dragging trucks along underground railway lines for up to 12 hours a day in the dark. Another important reform act in 1833 was the Abolition of Slavery in all the British Dominions.

THE TOLPUDDLE MARTYRS

Another issue that caused resentment among working people against the government and the ruling classes was the right to belong to a trade union. These were the new associations of workmen formed to protect their rights and wages in the new agricultural and industrial work places. The Combination Laws had made it unlawful to take an oath of allegiance to a union. In 1824 these laws were overturned by Parliament and trade unions were at last allowed. But a group of farmers and landowners found a loophole in the law and used it against the Tolpuddle Martyrs.

The Tolpuddle Martyrs were six labourers from Tolpuddle in Dorset who formed a trade union. They were tried for this, found guilty, and sentenced to seven years' transportation to Botany Bay in Australia. But there was such an outcry that they were pardoned and brought back in 1836. Five of them emigrated to Canada.

A year later William IV died, having reigned over a turbulent decade when many social evils were abolished and serious political reform began.

Left: **A Luddite protestor disguised in female clothes. The Luddites were craftworkers who opposed the new industrial machinery which they saw as a threat to their traditional jobs. Between 1811 and 1816 they smashed new machinery in factories in Lancashire. Six years later, a group of workers called the Blanketeers (because they wrapped themselves in the woollen cloth they wove), marched from Manchester to London to ask George, the Prince Regent, for help.**

Right: **There were many protests against the sentence given to the Tolpuddle Martyrs in 1834. Such protests led to their pardon in 1836.**

- **1834** Tolpuddle Martyrs deported to Australia. Fire destroys Houses of Parliament

- *c.* **1835** Terms Liberal and Conservative begin to replace Whig and Tory

- **1836** Civil marriages allowed for the first time. London University founded

- **1837** William IV dies. Succeeded by his niece, Victoria (to 1901)

RULERS OF BRITAIN

HOUSE	NAME	REIGN	MARRIED	CHILDREN
HANOVER	George I	1714 – 1727	Sophia of Brunswick	George II
	George II	1727 – 1760	Caroline of Anspach	Frederick Prince of Wales, William Duke of Cumberland
	George III (son of Frederick)	1760 – 1820	Charlotte-Sophia of Mecklenberg-Strelitz	Edward Duke of Kent, George IV, William IV
	George IV	1820 – 1830	Caroline of Brunswick	
	William IV	1830 – 1837	Adelaide of Saxe-Meiningen	

GLOSSARY

abolition ending of the slave trade

Act a law formally recorded in writing, resulting from a decision taken by Parliament

Agricultural Revolution changes in the 1700s in the use of farm machinery and sowing, planting and harvesting methods

aqueduct a bridge which carries canal boats on water, or the water supply

Baroque a style of music, art, architecture and sculpture which developed in western Europe from the late 16th century to the early 18th century. It aimed to produce spectacular and ornate effects.

bill a proposal to change or introduce a new law in Parliament that is debated and voted for or against (if passed, it becomes an Act)

blockade closing up of a place or country, by military or naval forces, generally to starve it into obedience or surrender

cabinet a small group of close advisers to the monarch; eventually this became a group who formed government policy

Catholics supporters and followers of the Church of Rome and the Pope

colony settlement by people settlers in new territory who are still subject to their country of origin

dissenters *see* **Non-Conformists**

dissolution dismissal of Parliament with a view to summoning a new one as and when the monarch required it

East India Company a trading company given monopoly of eastern trade by Elizabeth I in 1600. Later in conflict with Dutch East India Company

Georgian of the Hanoverian period; often used to label architecture of this time

Holy Roman Empire a federation of European states and princes, 800 to 1803

home secretary government minister responsible for police, prisons and conditions in factories

Industrial Revolution the changes that happened in the 1700s and 1800s as a result of the development of powered machinery and factories

Jacobite supporter of those who claimed the throne for the Stuart line of James II

Methodists followers of preacher John Welsey who believe in a very strict method of study and prayer

monopoly sole possession of, or control of trade in, any commodity

mutiny uprising by soldiers or sailors against their superiors

Non-Conformists those who do not agree with the established Church of England (including Catholics). Also called dissenters

Parliament highest body in Britain responsible for making laws, consisting of the House of Commons, the House of Lords and the sovereign

prime minister the most senior member of government and leader of the political party in power

Privy Council a body of people appointed for life by the sovereign to be the Crown's private councillors

Protestantism religion of any branch of the western Church separated from the Roman Catholic Church

Regency normally used to describe the period 1811-1820 when the Prince Regent (later George IV) ruled on behalf of his father George III, who had been declared insane. The term is also applied to the period's lavish style of architecture, interior design and fashion

rotten boroughs voting area which sent a member to Parliament despite the fact that hardly anyone lived there (while large new industrial towns had no MPs)

slave a person legally owned by another, without freedom or rights

statute a law or rule made by a body or institution, meant to be permanent and expressed in a formal document; especially an Act of Parliament

Tory member of the political party of the 19th century opposed to political reform, which evolved into the present-day Conservative party

Whig member of the political party of the 18th century favouring social and political reform, which evolved into the Liberal party

INDEX

ACKNOWLEDGMENTS

The publisher would like to thank the following for supplying additional illustrations for this book:

Picture research: Alex Goldberg, Elaine Willis

page 2, Walpole, Mark Peppé; p4, Bonnie Prince Charlie, Mark Peppé; p4, Sheriffmuir, e t archive; p6, Bank of England, Mark Peppé; p20, British Museum, Mark Peppé; p28, Pump Room, The Mansell Collection; p31, Polling Day, Sir John Soane's Museum